A NOTE TO PARENTS

When your children are ready to "step into reading," giving them the right books is as crucial as giving them the right food to eat. **Step into Reading Books** present exciting stories and information reinforced with lively, colorful illustrations that make learning to read fun, satisfying, and worthwhile. They are priced so that acquiring an entire library of them is affordable. And they are beginning readers with a difference— they're written on five levels.

Early Step into Reading Books are designed for brand-new readers, with large type and only one or two lines of very simple text per page. **Step 1 Books** feature the same easy-to-read type as the Early Step into Reading Books, but with more words per page. **Step 2 Books** are both longer and slightly more difficult, while **Step 3 Books** introduce readers to paragraphs and fully developed plot lines. **Step 4 Books** offer exciting nonfiction for the increasingly independent reader.

To Daniel Penner

Thanks to Dr. David Grimaldi
of the American Museum of Natural History
for his helpful advice.

Text copyright © 1996 by Lucille Recht Penner. Illustrations copyright © 1996 by Pamela Johnson. All rights reserved under International and Pan-American Copyright Conventions. Published in the United States by Random House, Inc., New York, and simultaneously in Canada by Random House of Canada Limited, Toronto.

Library of Congress Cataloging-in-Publication Data
Penner, Lucille Recht.
    Monster bugs / by Lucille Recht Penner ; illustrated by Pamela Johnson.
    p. cm. — (Step into reading. Step 2 book)
    Summary: Describes some of the world's largest insects, including the Goliath beetle, praying mantis, tarantula, and giant atlas moth.
    ISBN 0-679-86974-3 (pbk.) — ISBN 0-679-96974-8 (lib. bdg.)
    1. Insects—Juvenile literature. 2. Insects—Size—Juvenile literature. 3. Spiders—Juvenile literature. 4. Spiders—Size—Juvenile Literature. [1. Insects.] I. Johnson, Pamela, ill. II. Title. III. Series.
QL467.2.P458   1996   595.7—dc20   95-347

Printed in the United States of America 10 9 8 7 6 5 4 3 2
STEP INTO READING is a trademark of Random House, Inc.

Step into Reading

Monster Bugs

by Lucille Recht Penner

illustrated by Pamela Johnson

A Step 2 Book

Random House 🏠 New York

Have you ever
looked at a bug
<u>up close</u>?
You might see horns
or armor or spikes.
If bugs were your size,
they'd be scary.

No bug is as big as you.
But some are huge for bugs.
And some are fierce!
This book is all about
the biggest and fiercest bugs
in the world.

The heaviest bug
is the goliath beetle of Africa.
How heavy is it?
Get two eggs
out of the fridge.
Hold them together
in your hand.
That's how heavy
<u>one</u> goliath beetle is.

But goliath beetles
are gentle.
Some kids even keep them
as pets!

Not all beetles
are gentle.
The giant stag beetle
is a fighter!

These two beetles
are fighting over
a female.

One male grabs the other
in its huge jaws,
lifts it into the air,
and slams it down
on the ground!

A mouse wants to eat
this juicy bombardier beetle.
But the beetle
fires boiling-hot gas
from its rear end.

Bang! Bang! Bang!
Each burst explodes
like a firecracker.
The gas bombs
burn and sting,
and the mouse
runs away.

Giant waterbugs
stab their victims
and suck their blood
like vampires!

The mother waterbug
glues her eggs
to the father's back.
He carries them around
until they hatch.
Then, if the babies don't
swim away quickly,
he might eat them!

What's the stinkiest,
smelliest bug?
A stinkbug.

When a bird
scares a stinkbug,
the bug oozes
a horrible, smelly
liquid.

The bird flies away.
It doesn't want
a dinner
that stinks.

Australian
walking sticks
are the longest
of all bugs.
Hungry birds
love to eat them.

The walking stick
doesn't have big jaws
or burning gas
to fight with.
But it can
hold very still
and hide.
Look closely.
Can you see it
against this branch?

7   8   9   10   11   12

Some praying mantises
are as long as bananas.

This one jabs
a curious frog
with the spikes on its legs.
<u>Pow! Pow!</u>
The frog hops away.

A praying mantis
will eat anything
smaller than itself.
Even a baby bird
that falls from its nest.
After eating, the mantis
washes its face
like a kitten.

Army ants are killers.
Millions of them
march through the forest.

They eat anything
they can catch—
cockroaches, spiders, beetles,
and scorpions.

When they come
to a village,
even people hurry
to get out
of their way.

Grrrrrrr!
Imagine falling into
a lion's den.
It's happening
to these ants.
A hungry ant lion
has dug a pit.
It hides at the bottom,
buried in sand.
Only its powerful
jaws stick out.

When an ant falls in,
the ant lion grabs it,
sucks it dry,
and throws away the shell.

The body of a female,
black widow spider
is smaller than a dime,
but her poison
is stronger
than a rattlesnake's.

How did the
black widow
get its name?
Sometimes the female
spider kills and eats
her mate!

The raft spider
eats tadpoles
and little fish.

It stabs a minnow
with its deadly fangs,
pulls it
out of the water,
and gobbles it up.

Tarantulas are hairy spiders.
A big one would cover
your dinner plate.

Most tarantulas are gentle.
But some have
an unusual weapon—
their own hair.

When a coyote
tries to eat it,
the tarantula kicks
a cloud of itchy hairs
into the air.
The hairs make the coyote
cough and scratch.
Now the tarantula
can escape.

A tarantula's worst enemy
is a fierce wasp called
a tarantula hawk.

The spider tries to
fight off the wasp.
But the wasp darts in
and stings it.

Now the spider can't move.
The wasp drags it into its burrow
and lays an egg on it.
After the egg hatches,
the baby wasp
eats the tarantula alive.

Have you ever been
stung by a bee?
It hurts!

One bee sting
is bad enough.
But how about
hundreds of stings?
Killer bees are
smaller than other bees—
but a lot fiercer.
When they get mad,
they chase and sting
their enemies.

One man was stung
two thousand times!
A big dog
was stung to death.

The assassin bug
is another killer.

This assassin bug
is creeping up
on a caterpillar.
Suddenly it plunges
its sharp beak
into the caterpillar's
furry body.
Then it squirts in poison.
The caterpillar's insides
turn to mush.

The assassin bug
sucks up the mush
and goes hunting
for another meal.

A female horsefly
punctures the skin
of horses and cows
with her
sharp mouth parts.
Then she sucks
their blood.

In Africa
some horseflies
even suck the blood
of crocodiles!

Some moths
are as big
as birds.

If a giant atlas moth
sat <u>right here</u>,
its wings would
cover both pages.

The atlas moth is huge,
but it still has enemies.
How does it
protect itself?
Its wing tips look
like snake heads.
Most animals are
afraid of snakes.
They leave the moth alone.

How far can you
stick out your tongue?

The long-tongued
sphinx moth
has a tongue
eleven inches long.
That's four times
as long as its body.

If a ten-year-old boy
had a tongue like that,
it would be as long as
his mother's car!

Look at these
huge cockroaches!
Luckily, you won't
find them
in your kitchen.

Madagascar hissing
cockroaches
live on an island
near Africa.

If a bird grabs one,
the cockroach hisses loudly.
<u>Hsssssssssssssssss!</u>
The startled bird
drops the cockroach
and flies away.

Some millipedes
ooze poison
when they are
frightened.

Indians in Mexico
used to grind up
millipedes
to make a deadly poison.
Before a battle,
they rubbed the poison
on their arrows.

Most bugs won't
hurt you.
Bugs are important.
They are food
for many other
creatures.
And they help trees
and flowers grow.

Bugs keep
our planet clean
by eating dead plants
and animals.

We couldn't live
without bugs—
even the biggest,
scariest
monster bugs!